W9-CNS-872

A giant splash!

TWELVE jittery jellyfish
shivered and shook
with the spectacular splash.

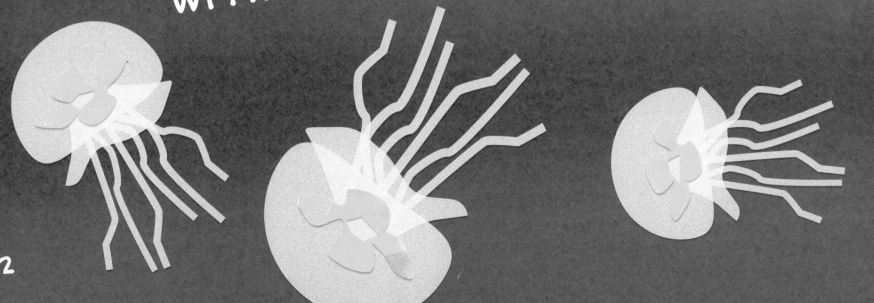

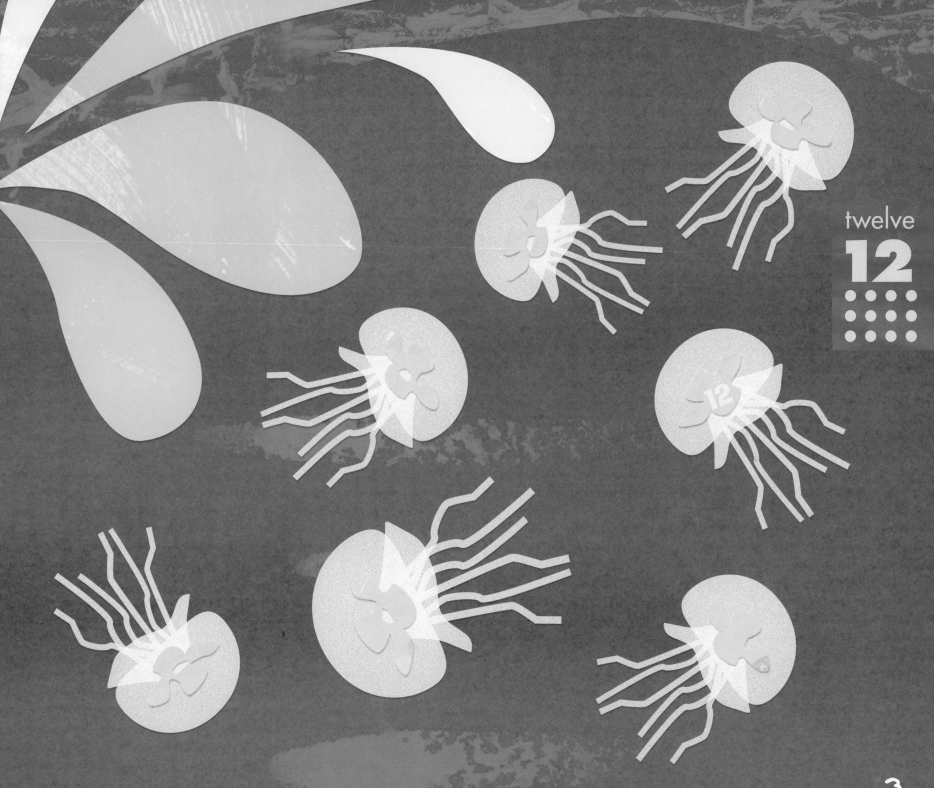

twelve

12

3

ELEVEN salty shrimp somersaulted through the sky.

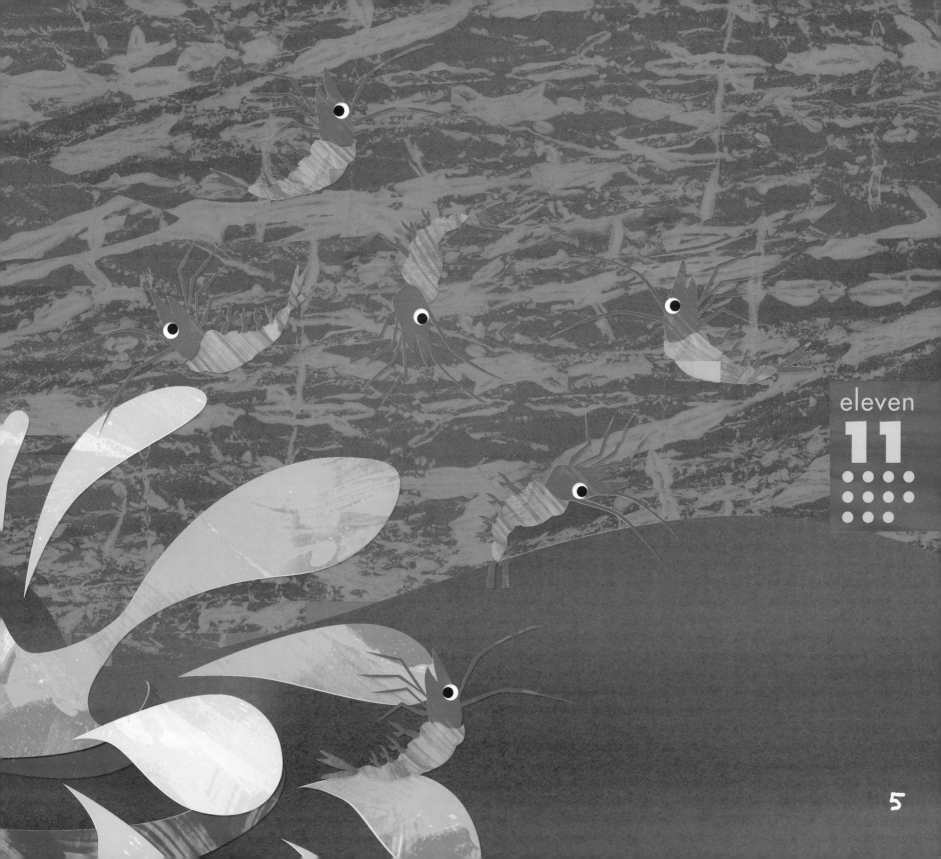

eleven
11
· · · ·
· · · ·
· · ·

5

TEN excited eels made wiggles above the waves.

ten
10

7

NINE startled sharks slipped swiftly down to silent water.

nine

9

9

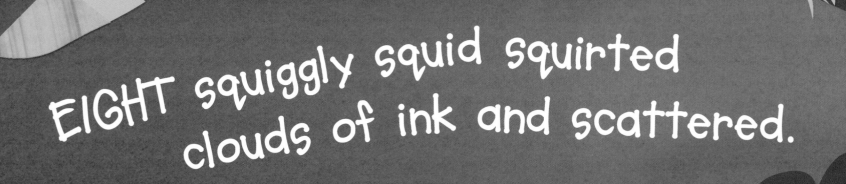

EIGHT squiggly squid squirted clouds of ink and scattered.

SEVEN astounded stingrays stuck
and stung one another.

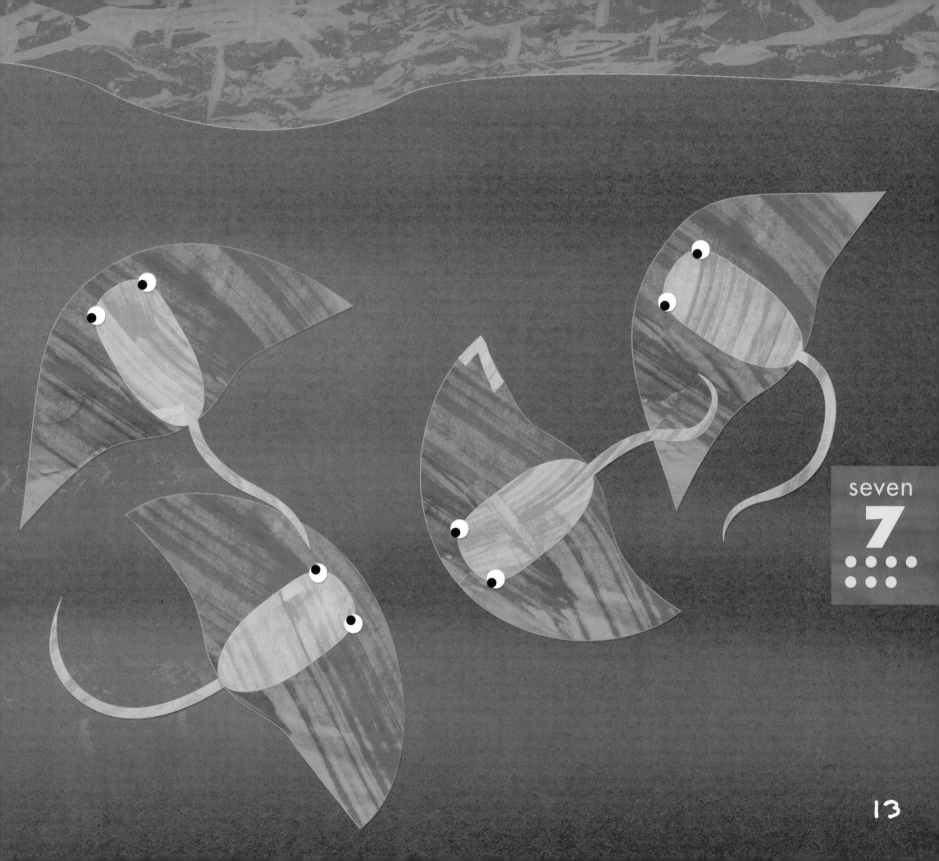

seven
7
● ● ● ●
● ● ●

13

six
6

SIX curious crabs scuttled toward the sandy shore.

FIVE flabbergasted flounders flopped
and flipped and flew about.

five
5
:···:

FOUR bewildered walruses bellowed and blew through their snouts.

four
4
● ● ● ●

THREE delighted dolphins danced
on the dazzling waves.

TWO slippery seals bounced
and bumped and barked with glee.

two

2

18

But who made the giant splash?

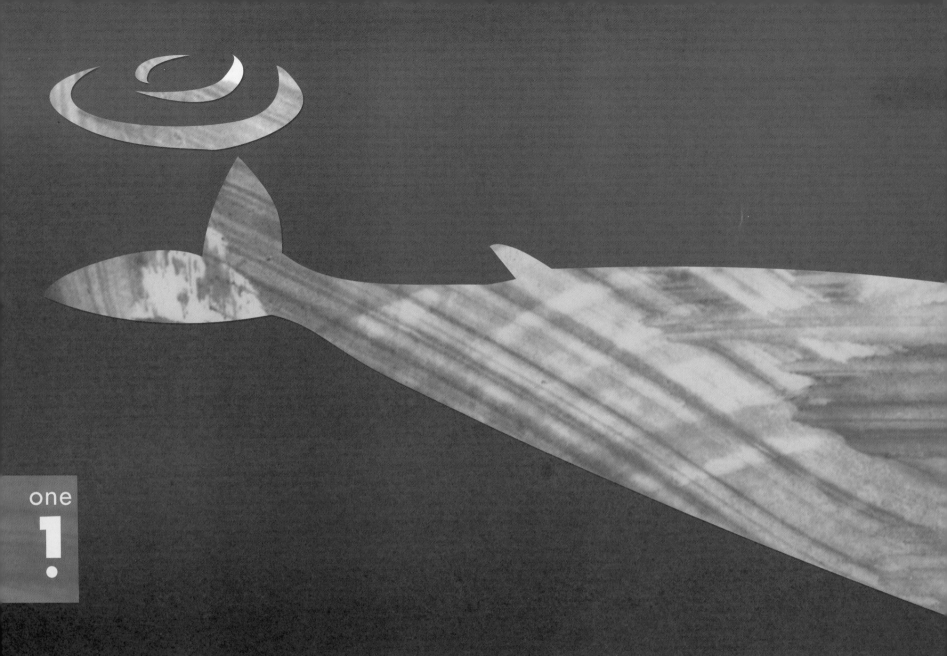

one
!

20

ONE big blue whale.

Fun Facts

	jellyfish	A jellyfish swims by pushing its body out and pulling it back in, kind of like an umbrella opens and closes.
	shrimp	Most shrimp have 19 pairs of legs!
	eel	Young eels are great swimmers. Some are so strong, they can climb waterfalls and dams!
	shark	All sharks are meat-eaters. Some sharks even eat other sharks.
	squid	A squid can change the color and pattern of its body to blend in with the world around it. This helps protect the squid from its enemies.
	stingray	There are about 100 different kinds of stingrays. Most live on the muddy or sandy bottoms of bays and oceans.
	crab	A crab's body is covered with a shell called a carapace. The shell helps protect the crab.
	flounder	There are more than 300 different kinds of flounders. Flounders are a group of flatfishes that live in saltwater.
	walrus	A walrus has four flat feet called flippers. The flippers help the walrus move easily through the water.
	dolphin	The bottle-nosed dolphin is the most well-known kind of dolphin. It can grow up to 13 feet (4 meters) long and weigh about 600 pounds (272 kilograms)!
	seal	Seals close their noses when they swim underwater. This keeps water from going into their noses.
	blue whale	The blue whale is the biggest animal that has ever lived on Earth.

Find the Numbers

Now you have finished reading the story, but a surprise still awaits you.

Hidden in each picture is one of the numbers from 1 to 12. Can you find them all?

Key

12—inside the body of the jellyfish in the center of the farthest right row

11—on the shrimp second from the right

10—on the eel in the top right corner

9—in the splash at the top of the page

8—in the ink from the lowest squid on page 11

7—on the stingray second from right

6—on the crab in the center of the bottom row

5—on the fin of the flounder in the center of the bottom row

4—on the left tooth of the walrus on the bottom left

3—in the splash in front of the dolphin that is farthest right

2—the ear of the left seal

1—near the whale's front fin

Go on an Observation Walk

Counting is fun! Step outside your door, and practice counting by going on an observation walk in your neighborhood—or even in your own yard. Ask an adult to go with you. On an observation walk, you notice the things all around you. Count the number of trees in your yard or on your block. Count the number of dogs you see. Count the number of windows on one side of your home. You can count everything!

Glossary

eel—a fish that looks like a snake

jellyfish—a sea animal that has a soft, almost clear body and tentacles. A jellyfish is shaped like an umbrella.

squid—a sea creature that has 10 tentacles attached to a long, soft body

stingray—a fish that has a flat body, fins that look like wings, and a long, poisonous tail

Index

On the Web

Fact Hound
Fact Hound offers a safe, fun way to find Web sites related to this book. All of the sites on Fact Hound have been researched by our staff.
http://www.facthound.com

1. Visit the Fact Hound home page.
2. Enter a search word related to this book, or type in this special code:140480577X.
3. Click on the FETCH IT button.

Your trusty Fact Hound will fetch the best sites for you!

Acknowledgments

Thanks to our advisers for their expertise, research, and advice:

Stuart Farm, M.A.
Mathematics Lecturer,
University of North Dakota
Grand Forks, North Dakota

Susan Kesselring, M.A.
Literacy Educator
Rosemount-Apple Valley-Eagan
(Minnesota) School District

The editor would like to thank Samantha Norton, coordinator of School Programs at John G. Shedd Aquarium, for her expert advice in preparing this book.

Managing Editor: Bob Temple
Creative Director: Terri Foley
Editor: Brenda Haugen
Editorial Adviser: Andrea Cascardi
Copy Editor: Sue Gregson
Designer: Nathan Gassman
Page production: Picture Window Books

The illustrations in this book were rendered digitally.

Picture Window Books
5115 Excelsior Boulevard
Suite 232
Minneapolis, MN 55416
1-877-845-8392
www.picturewindowbooks.com

Copyright © 2004 by
Picture Window Books
All rights reserved. No part of this book may be reproduced without written permission from the publisher. The publisher takes no responsibility for the use of any of the materials or methods described in this book, nor for the products thereof.

Printed in the United States of America.

Library of Congress Cataloging-in-Publication Data
Dahl, Michael.
　　One giant splash : a counting book about the ocean /
　　written by Michael Dahl ;
　　illustrated by Todd Ouren.
　　p. cm. — (Know your numbers)
　　Includes bibliographical
　　references and index.
　　Summary: Uses marine animals, such as twelve jellyfish and two seals, to count down from twelve to one.
　　ISBN 1-4048-0577-X (reinforced lib. bdg.)
　1. Counting—Juvenile literature.
　2. Marine animals—Juvenile literature.
　[1. Counting. 2. Marine animals.]
　I. Ouren, Todd, ill. II. Title.
QA113.D34 2004
513.2'11—dc22
　　　　　　　　　　　　　　　2003020929